Discover Back to School

© Xist Publishing 2012
Hardcover ISBN: 978-1-5324-3702-1
Paperback ISBN: 9781623955946
eISBN: 9781623952969
Images licensed from Fotolia.com
First Edition
Published in the United States by Xist
Publishing
www.xistpublishing.com

xist Publishing

This is a three-hole punch.

Teachers use them to make holes in paper so you can put them in a binder.

These are art supplies.
You can create fun projects
with them.

This is a backpack.
You will bring your lunch and
homework in your backpack, then
you will hang it on a hook.

This is a pen.
Pens are used to write dark lines.

These are binder clips.
Teachers use them to hold stacks of paper together.

This is construction paper.
Teachers cut and tear it for art projects.

These are crayons.
You can use crayons to color pictures.

13

This is a globe.
Globes show all of the countries in the world.

This is a highlighter.
Teachers use highlighters to show important words.

These are markers.

You can use markers to color pictures.

These are pencils.
Each has a number two on it to
show how hard and dark it is.

These are notebooks.
You can write in them and keep your papers inside.

This is a pencil and eraser.

Pencil marks can be erased
or removed.

This is a pencil pouch.

You will be able to keep pencils, pens, and other school supplies in your pencil pouch.

This is a pencil sharpener.
It is hard to write with a dull pencil.
A pencil sharpener will make your
pencil have a sharp point.

This is a push pin.
Teachers use push pins to hang papers on the wall.

These are rubber bands.
Teachers will use them to hold papers.

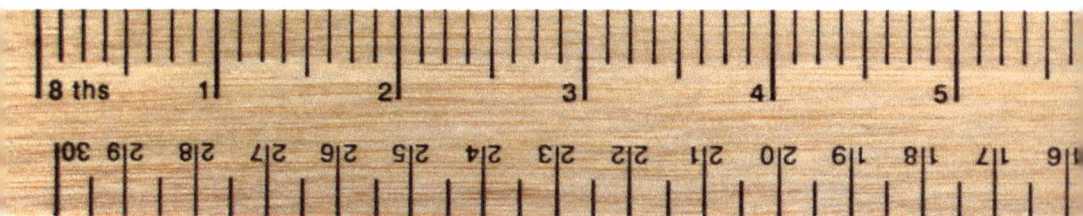

This is a ruler.
You will use a ruler to
measure small items.

This is a roll of tape.
Tape is sticky and can be used on paper, walls, and skin.

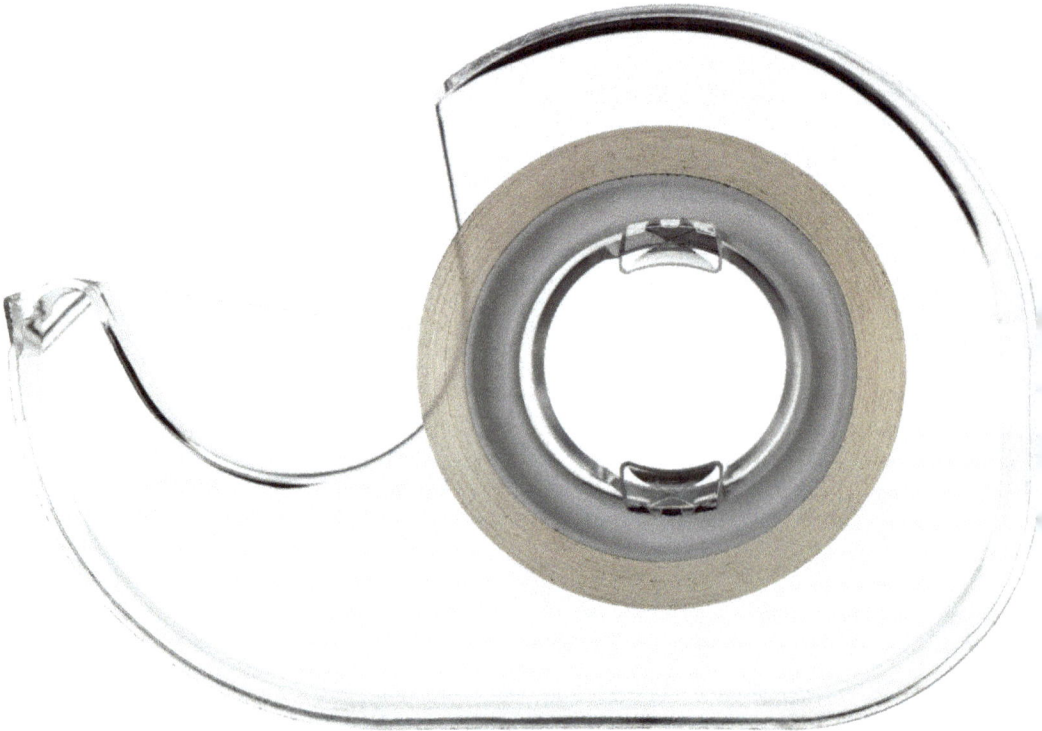

This is a stapler.

It uses small pieces of metal to hold papers together.

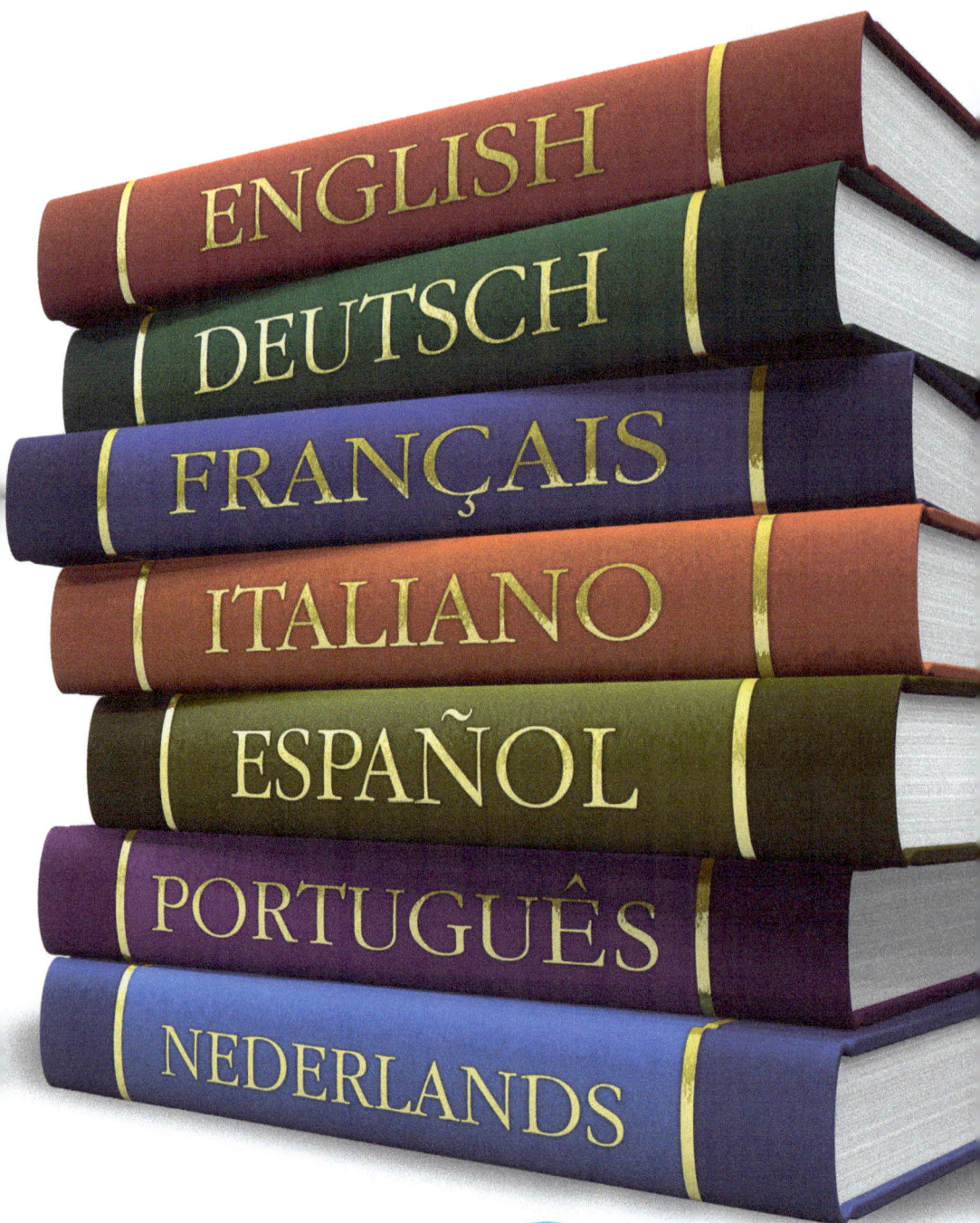

ENGLISH

DEUTSCH

FRANÇAIS

ITALIANO

ESPAÑOL

PORTUGUÊS

NEDERLANDS

These are text books.
You will use text books to learn with the rest of the class.

This is a school bus.

You may walk, drive, or ride a bus to school. You will ride a bus when you go on field trips.

35

www.ingramcontent.com/pod-product-compliance
Lightning Source LLC
Chambersburg PA
CBHW040417110426
42813CB00013B/2682